LIFE AND IDEOLOGY

OF

SREE SREE ANUKULCHANDRA

A brief sketch

Dr. Srikumar Mukherjee

MSc | MA | PhD

Life and Ideology of Sree Sree Anukulchandra: *A brief sketch*
Copyright © Srikumar Mukherjee
All rights reserved.
1st Edition: September 14, 2020
2nd Edition: January 26, 2025
Cover design: Samrat Chatterjee
ISBN: **9798897775583**

An
IndoAryan School of Human Resource Development (ISHRD)
Publication
In association with Notion Press and Amazon

Price Rs 150 ($ 15.99)

Dedicated to:

Rev. Shri Bidyut Ranjan Chakraborty

Grandson of Sree Sree Anukulchandra
(*Adhyaksha,* PSSAC, Bibek Bitan, Deoghar)

*"Goal of life is God realisation, or in
other words – attainment of a personality in which
the urge of upholding and protecting others,
is firmly established;
The means to it is active adherence to the Ideal,
and from this flow self-adjustment,
adjustment of the family, society and the state;
and from this adjustment of the state begins
advancement towards becoming –
forgoing a link with the whole world,
and therefrom springs the urge to find fulfilment of
everything in God;
and this is the supreme consciousness of -
God-realisation."*

---Sree Sree Anukulchandra

Contains

"Cultivate culture

The field is vast

Cultivators are few

Be one of them"

---Sree Sree Anukulchandra

Introduction

Modern human civilisation is marked by unprecedented scientific advancement alongside deepening existential distress. Despite remarkable progress in technology, economics, and political organisation, individuals and societies continue to struggle with meaninglessness, alienation, psychological disorder, social fragmentation, and ecological imbalance. Classical materialist explanations—whether economic, political, or technological—have demonstrated limited capacity to address these multidimensional crises of human existence.

My own intellectual journey began within this tension. Influenced initially by dialectical materialism and Marxist critiques of religion, I approached social reality through a rationalist and anti-metaphysical framework. Religious belief, ritual practice, and the notion of God appeared incompatible with scientific reasoning and social emancipation. In this phase, Dharma was perceived largely as a non-material abstraction, sustained by faith rather than reason.

However, a critical turning point emerged through engagement with diverse philosophical, religious, and sociological traditions—including the Gita, Buddhism, Christianity, Islam, and the works of modern Indian thinkers. This comparative inquiry revealed a persistent disjunction between the core insights of spiritual traditions and their ritualistic or institutionalised expressions. While scriptures themselves did not inherently promote communalism or social stagnation, their lived practices often failed to address the real causes of human suffering.

It was in this context that I encountered the life and thought of Sree Sree Anukulchandra (1888–1969). What distinguished Him sociologically was not formal education or institutional authority, but a distinctive capacity to articulate existential problems in rational, experiential, and pragmatic terms. His interpretations of Dharma, existence, and consciousness were neither mystical abstractions nor theological dogma, but appeared as functional explanations of human life rooted in observable psychological and social processes.

Central to His thought was a redefinition of Dharma—not as ritual obligation or belief in a supernatural deity, but as the science of being and becoming, that is, the process by which living entities sustain existence while evolving through harmonious interaction with their environment. Within this framework, "God" is not a metaphysical entity external to life, but the existential urge inherent in matter itself—the impulse toward preservation, growth, and integration. This conception provided a rational bridge between materialism and spirituality, allowing both to be understood as complementary dimensions of a single evolutionary process.

Through prolonged engagement with His teachings, social practices, and institutional experiments, it became evident that Sree Sree Anukulchandra was not merely a religious leader but a systemic thinker whose ideas encompassed psychology, education, sociology, ecology, and human development. His emphasis on Initiation, Education, and Marriage Reform emerged as a structured Human Resource Development (HRD) model aimed at addressing individual pathology and societal degeneration simultaneously.

This work is therefore not intended as devotional literature, nor as theological advocacy. Rather, it is a sociological and philosophical inquiry into the life and ideology of Sree Sree Anukulchandra, examined as a modern civilisational response to the crisis of human existence. Drawing upon fieldwork, textual analysis, and comparative theory, the study seeks to interpret His contribution as an integrated existential framework—here termed 'IndoAryan Existentialism'—which attempts to reconcile material progress with spiritual consciousness, individual freedom with social order, and scientific rationality with ethical responsibility.

The purpose of presenting this work in a concise form is to invite critical engagement rather than unquestioned acceptance. If the ideas explored here stimulate inquiry into the fundamental question of human existence—how to be, how to become, and how to live in harmony with the whole—then the effort may be considered meaningful within the larger continuum of human thought.

Srikumar Mukherjee
September 14, 2020

Email: srikumar.hrm@gmail.com
Phone: +91-8210137153
Website: www.indoaryan.in

Life sketch of Sree Sree Anukulchandra:

On September 14, 1888, about 1.5 centuries ago, a boy was born in a lower-middle-class Bengali Brahmin family at Himayetpur village of Pabna district of undivided Bengal, now in Bangladesh, before the Partition (1947 AD) of India. He was named Anukulchandra, after his mother, Monmohini Devi. He was given spiritual indoctrination by his mother following the direction of her Guru – Sarkar Sahab (disciple of Huzur Maharaj, founder of *Radhaswami* Satsang). The divine faculty was powerfully manifested in Anukulchandra right from His childhood, which made itself evident in the proverbial comment that he knew this 'Name' since the very beginning, and it was not new to him. Through rigorous spiritual practice and unwavering devotion, he began to realise his integral inner relationship with the whole creation. He assumed that there is no difference between matter and spirit, and every matter is conscious because it gives and receives impulses, but its level differs from matter to matter. This experience made him deeply inquisitive about his environment, and he inferred that everyone primarily loves their existence to evolve further, but this becoming is coterminous with their environment also. Put baldly, nourishment to the environment to fulfil self-existence is called *Dharma*. He believes that sustaining one's existence is intertwined with caring for the environment, and this nurturing relationship is the essence of Dharma. So, according to Him, *Dharma* is not without the paraphernalia of science. This all-pervading spirit brings true awareness of total existence, which culminates in attaining the state of becoming, i.e. salvation or *Brahma-Darsan*.

His inquisitive childhood was very concentric on his mother, and he left no stone unturned to keep up with the expectations of the latter. By continuously maintaining the verve, his boyhood mind used to be engaged in meditation to reveal the secret laws of nature and to understand the cause of the plight in which the common humanity was mired. He used to search for a small plant's life cycle in the garden. He detected that plants maintain their uniqueness and there are dissimilarities within the same type of objects, and He concluded that there is no apparent resemblance in nature. He mesmerised people with his ingenuity and attention to detail. Once, after travelling by steamer with his father, he built a steam engine at home. He also successfully shaped a wooden stick into a fountain pen. One day, He treated one of his young friends suffering from stomach pain by giving him a locally available herb to eat. Quite interestingly, by tasting the same herb, he once suffered from stomach pain with similar symptoms of his friend. He revealed, "During my adulthood, I found that the formula of Heinemann - the father of Homoeopathy medicine, was similar to what I discovered and experienced at an early age."

Despite struggling with poverty, Anukulchandra's relationship with the people around him was deep and cordial because he was trying to be closer to the villagers. Anukulchandra had shown his quest quite palpably with his mission – how to deal with the people and how to rescue them from their physical void. He said about his deeds of those days - "I got the answer when I found in one of the writings in my school's exercise book - *Do unto others as you wish to be done!*" The annals of events in his lifetime attest to his missionary benevolence, and these were evident in the way that most of the paranoid and obsessed people were converted into normal human beings with his sympathetic and loving nourishment, and he began appropriating the Image of a Redeemer with his espousal of the causes and sufferings of humanity.

Anukulchandra studied at the high school of Pabna but could not matriculate. His school career was discontinued when he offered his board examination fees to one of his poor friends. After that, he went to Calcutta to study at a medical school. While studying medicine, he gathered lots of experience in medicine, which enabled him to formulate his future course of action. Being a student from a lower-middle-class family, he had gathered intimate knowledge of the sufferings of life because he stayed for years with the labourers at a coal depot. He had to pass many days without food, but only water from the roadside drinking water tap and spend nights at railway platforms. Finally, he returned to his village without any medical diploma, because he was asked to reappear in the final practical examination. Within a very short period, he became very popular and a very busy medical practitioner in his village. During that period, he noticed that those who were getting cured by medicine often visited him with the same disease. He perceived that the indisposition of the patients is caused more by mental disposition than by their physical debilitations. So, he decided that the patients had to be treated with sense, intellect, spirit, and compassion.

Then he introduced *'Kirtan'* – a group devotional song sung with the indigenous musical instruments, among the village-dwellers with high pitch, to heal their obsessed mind. In his words, "The tune of his melodious *Kirtan* uplifts people's mind to higher esteem very rapidly." This divine sound brought a huge response from people belonging to the far-flung districts of Bengal. While *Kirtan* used to reach its ultimate melodious crescendo, sometimes Anukulchandra would become unconscious and lose almost all of the signs and insignia of life, and it continued for hours, having only 'divine' words on his lips. This state is popularly known as *'Samadhi'*. At this stage of his existence, he used to utter different subject matters such as the way of life, techniques on control over passions, the mystery of the creation of nature, spiritual realisations, salvation, solutions of many individual and social matters in the Bengali language as well as English, Hindi, Sanskrit and some other unknown languages. People flocked in great numbers, and they were irradiated with a divine glow emanating from the utterances of Anukulchandra. With time, people from other parts of the country were attracted to him. Anukulchandra frequently underwent the state of *Samadhi,* out of which only 72 days had been recorded and later published at *'Punyaputhi'* (Holy Book), and the rest of these days could not be noted. The medical explanation of these periods of his life is yet to be excavated. Since then, Anukulchandra has been popularly known as Sree Sree Thakur Anukulchandra.

He observed closely that the people are getting mentally charged by *Kirtan,* but are unable to retain the emotion for a long period. He concluded that people's emotional attachment to the higher and pure idea is the only way to harmonise the complications, and that which can only rescue one from physical and mental disease.

Now, Sree Sree Anukulchandra concentrated on social reformation by building the character of the people. He translated his vision by introducing three structural programs to metamorphose the nation. The first is 'Initiation', i.e., a 'man-making' program for each individual to realise the goal of the psycho-sexual attachment with a higher Ideal person. The second is 'Education' with the desire to follow the path of unfolding good instincts with Ideal-centric guidance. The third is 'Marriage' with a vision to apply the genetic evolution (law of genetic-lift of nature) to transmitting the good characteristics to the next generations. Keeping this tripartite structural innovation in mind, He initiated a massive program on psycho-spiritual treatment, family adjustment, educational reformation, health hygiene, genetic-refinement, industry, agriculture, scientific research, publicity, etc. People belonging to the multifarious classes and professions and representing different walks and parts of the country and abroad came to him to find the solutions to their varied quests in their journey of life. Sree Sree Anukulchandra introduced *Ritwik-Sangha* with the selected spiritually elevated devotees, who would execute His idea and program by transmitting the spirit into the slumbered humanity to reach them to the state of becoming and to wither away the existential dilemma. Gradually, this took the shape of an organised movement – popularly known as "Satsang-Movement".

The Satsang organisation was born and given a niche under the aegis of Sree Sree Anukulchandra with a missionary zeal, considering the demanding circumstances of His popularity. The rudimentary purpose of the Satsang organisation was to carry forward and execute the teachings of Sree Sree Anukulchandra with an arduous spirit to uphold world humanity. The most remarkable programmatic action of the Satsang movement in the backdrop of socio-economic and political scenarios was to build the plinth of communal harmony, cultural development, and modern scientific awareness based on traditional thoughts. Upholding the idea of the fulfilling life and ideology of the past prophets like Krishna, Buddha, Jesus, Mohammad, Chaitanya, Ramakrishna, etc., He said that the true follower of one's own prophet never becomes communal. The most amazing aspect was that tens of thousands of religious followers from different religions accepted Sree Sree Anukulchandra as a Master or 'Guru' and assembled to imbibe the divine spirit with the singular intention of making themselves a better spiritual practitioner of their respective faith and rational complete human being.

By the time the Satang movement was gaining momentum, Bengal was undergoing a very turbulent period, with the stoking of communal tension reaching its state of febrile intoxication. A spate of violent incidents begins to brew and rears its ugly head. The imminence of the Partition of India was then a matter of time. In this crucial period, the sagacious faculty in Sree Sree Anukulchandra prompted Him to launch a program for equalising the ratio of the population of Hindus and Muslims to resist the forthcoming dismemberment of India. He also appealed to the contemporary political giants who came to meet Him for support, to give primary importance to His cause to thwart the evil designs of some political leaders with vested interests to divide India into communal lines. Ironically, He received nothing but assurance and opposition as well. He also stumbled upon a plethora of obstacles from the local Hindu landlords to implement His programs. The political turmoil left a deep impact on Him, and finally, He had to leave His abode of institutions and properties, which He had meticulously cared to take shape and grow up to better the conditions of the suffering humanity. His institutions and properties in East Bengal include Tapovan School, Mata Monmohini College, Vishwa Vigyan Kendra (Scientific Research Centre), Press, Workshop, Hospital, Laundry, Agricultural Fields, etc. Md. Alam Hossein, an old farmer at Himayetpur village standing at the front of his cottage said in an interview (to the author in 1996) "The fields you can see so far was of Thakur!" He cried and said, "There was no problem till He stayed here, He was our messenger of Allah!" After leaving East Bengal, Sree Sree Anukulchandra settled in Deoghar of Santhal Pargana district of Bihar (now in Jharkhand state in India) and made His permanent abode there on 2nd September 1946. Barely one year after His settlement in Deoghar, India was divided in 1947 with heavy bloodshed and casualties of life, and His Pabna *Ashram* was severed from India and included in East Pakistan (now in Bangladesh).

After the Partition of India, the Satsang movement took its shape differently under His guidance, assuming multifarious proportions. The refugees from East Pakistan were given shelter and support in Satsang Ashram at Deoghar, and Sree Sree Anukulchandra personally took special care to provide immediate relief to them. To tackle the post-partition grave scenario and stave off the suffering of humanity slipping into a state of degeneration, He emphasised the organised movement on social change throughout the States based on three charters aligning with the non-communal agenda, viz. Initiation, Education, and Marriage-Reform. Millions of people responded to His clarion call. Many people from Europe, America, and other continents also accepted Him as a spiritual guide to becoming a pure Christian, Muslim, or Hindu. Now his initiation is getting spread over the world day by day, whose official number is about seven crores today.

In the early morning of 27th January 1969, the 'God' of the devotees, the Master of the followers, 'Super genius' for the knowledge seekers, 'Most loving sympathiser' for the common people, Sree Sree Anukulchandra passed away, leaving behind His humanitarian works and substantial ideological contribution towards the World human society. Once He said – "Everything has been given in my prose and poetry, I believe anybody who wants, can talk to me, even when I am not present......I have given you an everlasting torch, using it beyond may be achieved." The research found it as a key to the quest for human life. Let's have a look at those key points.

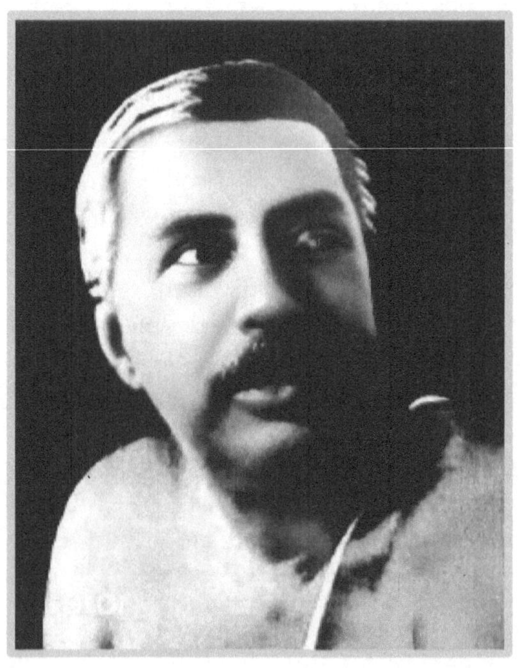

An Overview:

This work presents a concise sociological and philosophical exposition of the life and ideology of Sree Sree Anukulchandra (1888–1969), interpreting his contribution not as devotional theology but as an integrated existential framework addressing the modern crisis of human civilisation. Positioned against the backdrop of rapid scientific advancement accompanied by psychological, social, and ecological disintegration, the study examines Anukulchandra's thought as a rational, experiential, and systemic response to the problem of human existence.

Central to the ideology of Sree Sree Anukulchandra is a redefinition of Dharma—not as religion or ritual, but as the science of being and becoming, the universal law through which life sustains itself and evolves in harmony with its environment. Within this framework, 'God' is not conceived as a supernatural entity but as the 'existential urge' inherent in matter, driving preservation, growth, integration and consciousness. This formulation provides a conceptual bridge between materialism and spiritualism, presenting them as complementary dimensions of a single evolutionary process to bring all schools of thought onto one platform in terms of Existentialism, what he says - 'Root of all isms is Existentialism, no existence, no ism.'

This work outlines Anukulchandra's holistic model of Human Resource Development (HRD), structured around three interrelated pillars: Initiation, Education, and Marriage Reform.

Initiation is understood as a psycho-spiritual process of Ideal-centric attachment, enabling the systematic adjustment of human complexes. Education is defined as the disciplined organisation of instincts and habits to unfold innate potentialities and social responsibility. Marriage Reform is proposed as a scientifically guided process of psychogenic and genetic compatibility aimed at improving individual stability and generational continuity. Together, these form an integrated mechanism for individual transformation and social regeneration.

From a sociological perspective, the work situates Anukulchandra within a lineage of world teachers—such as Rama, Krishna, Buddha, Christ, and Muhammad—while emphasising his relevance to contemporary global challenges. His thought extends to theories of social organisation, division of labour based on instinctive aptitude, socio-environmental ecology (SEE), and the vision of a Divine Global Society, where material progress, ethical responsibility, and ecological balance are harmonised.

The article further articulates 'IndoAryan Existentialism' as a universal civilisational paradigm grounded in existential inquiry, scientific rationality, and moral integration. Rather than advocating communal, racial, or political ideology, it proposes a silent, non-confrontational cultural transformation aimed at cultivating conscious individuals capable of sustaining a balanced global order.

Overall, this executive study positions Sree Sree Anukulchandra as a modern existential thinker whose integrated approach to psychology, education, social reform, and spirituality offers a coherent theoretical framework for addressing the enduring question of human existence: how to be, how to become, and how to live in harmony with the whole.

Quest of Life:

The purpose of life is to uphold existence and to sustain continuous evolution with a realisation of 'oneness' with the whole. This evolutionary process gives birth to a human being. His apparent existential becoming continues until he realises his inner relationship with the mechanism of the whole environment. This awareness of self-existence makes human beings conscious of their surroundings for a better existence and infinite material, mental, intellectual, and spiritual progress. This inquisitiveness towards laws of existential-becoming of life makes his mind research-oriented, seeking peace, prosperity, enjoyment, happiness, and salvation (i.e. free from obsessions of complexes). This journey starts with the quest of life – 'Who am I, and how am I related to the whole in terms of evolution, since the beginning of creation?' This inquisitive mind explores the source, which he can attach himself to identify his complexes. And that attachment gives an impulse to make him aware of manipulating those complexes in favour of a better existence. So, he seeks to love a man or matter or material for his attachment, which may resolve his quest for life.

The root of all ism-s is 'Existentialism':

The struggle for existence has made the evolution of human society ever-active. So, the root of all physical, economic, cultural, social, intellectual, and spiritual activities is only for existential enjoyment. This finally brings control over the existential factors out of the 'urge of existence', which may be called 'God-realization', and that brings 'salvation'. Salvation is nothing but realising the mechanism of Socio-Environmental-Ecology (SEE) by gaining gradual mastery over being freed and exorcised from the obsession. From the primitive age of human society, it was rightly denominated as "early communism" – when human beings intellectually developed through a struggle for survival. After they evolved, their 'desire for existence' didn't remain the only desire so far. Now human beings undertake a journey to search for a better way of living. Thus, the 'desire for becoming' also became the inevitable and inalienable part of life, along with the 'desire of being'. Since then, their wanting to be and become made them reformed by gradually adjusting their complexes. The Master Sree Sree Anukulchandra says, "...the wants of enjoying life or the desire of existence is the driving factor of evolution." The inference is that cultural and biological ways of the incessant evolution of individuals collectively transform into social evolution.

The building unit of society is the human being. Scientifically, human is described as "sexual" as well as "creative" animals. The 'creativity' only makes humans different from the animal kingdom. The Master has devised three programmatic schemes, picked from the characteristics and factors of the course of social evolution for 'Human Resource Development' (HRD). That shows the solution to the crisis of the 'degeneration of humanity' of civilisation by applying both of those human qualities: 'creativity' and 'sexuality'. Those three points are - **(1)** Accepting Ideal ideal-centric disciplined life, called 'Initiation', **(2)** Complex adjustment training to extract the inborn potential called 'Education', and **(3)** Better progeny by 'Marriage-Reform'. **Firstly**, having 'Initiation' of a superior guide, one lovingly follows his master and happily adjusts himself according to his guidance with activity. The Father of Human Psychology, Freud says this in his own terms - "Psycho-sexual attachment to a psychologist", the man of the balanced and adjusted complex, is the prime factor of psychic treatment (i.e. adjustment of complexes). **Secondly**, 'Education' is a self-development process under the guidance of a master-man and practising to invest the urge of complexes for being and becoming. **Thirdly**, 'Marriage-reform' is a psychogenic matching of females and males for 'self-becoming' and 'better offspring', which would be the most valuable asset of the society. Thus, Initiation and Education develop the 'Creativity' for becoming and also teach to manipulate 'Sexuality' through Marriage-Reform for procuring more creative and efficient instinct. To conclude, we understand that - if there is no want of existence, there is no existence of life, viz., the root of all isms is existentialism, and the ideology appeared as the quintessential medium for human existence.

Evolution of Human Society:

The advent of man was a milestone in the process of evolution. When he had first thrown the stone or extended his hand using a branch of a tree to protect himself or to collect food, this was the use of the first machine and application of intelligence of mind, and it was the first step of the transition from animal to man. Now this man had developed a new dimension – the 'psychological unit' within himself, along with its 'biological unit'. At present, genetically, man is only 1.2% superior to his prior animal Chimpanzee, which (small genetic difference) makes such a big morphological, cultural, and genetic variation. In the course of cultural and social development, out of their own free choice, instinctively (inner desire according to its psychogenic getup), human beings had opted for different sections of occupations in cultivation. Thus, society was broadly grouped into four divisions: 'Research and development', 'Managerial and administrative', 'Business and economy', and 'Labour and service', which evolved naturally for better social management. From then onwards, it was no longer just an occupation, but an adaptation of respective occupations that became the hereditary character. Now, different families willingly absorbed into this occupation and converted into experts in these occupations.

Primarily, this distribution of work became an essential thing for better social management in all corners of the globe. Thus, the normal emergence of such a division of labour in a revolutionary manner progressively changed the social structure. Initially, people had chosen different contemporary trades freely according to their tastes (biological bent). But as we had observed by cultivating the same trade liberally through generation after generation, they became experts in those specific trades by acquiring the respective characters even bio-culturally (genetically). Thus, in society, the "division of labour according to hereditary instinct" was established. Nesfield says – "Occupation is the only factor of this system (caste)", whereas Dezil Ibbison says – "This is not sudden, but a product of a long process of evolution, and occupation became heredity." According to the Seer of the Age, "This is not a man-made system, but a universal law of the division of biological character, which could be found everywhere in nature." He termed this system in human society as "Grouping of society according to biological instinct." In his view, to put it elaborately, it was broadly divided into four natures of work, and those are - **Intellectual**, **Managerial**, **Commercial**, and **Physical** labour, as we have seen before, found in every society of the world in different forms and manifestations. In Indo-Aryan society, these natures of grouping were defined by the Seers as the Evolutionary division of social labour (*Varna*) - in terms of Bipra (hereditarily Brahmin), Kshatriya, Vaishya, and Sudra respectively. In this Indo-Aryan society, 'to be a Brahmin' was set as the 'goal of all'.

Now, by cultivating the existential culture of the people under the guidance of Seers and managing the marriage of the females (with the males of higher cultural heredity, often called *Varna*, they were gradually developing their hereditary characters to be promoted into the highest level of functional-instinctive grouping (*Varna*). This was set as one of the prime goals of this instinctive grouping to make everyone a hereditary-Brahmin (*Bipra*). But over a long course of time, due to some socio-cultural mismanagement, the rational image of this scientific social system had declined sharply, and instead of reforming the minor drawbacks, it was blacklisted in the name of 'dirty caste-differences!' This is a big step of ignorance!

A report is published on Anthropological and genetic research jointly organised by an Indo-US University team on the Indo-Aryan traditional *Varna* (caste) division system, which attests to the veracity of this system (*Varna*). The report says that still, these characters have been inherited through DNA for more than the past 3000 years. In the 'hypergamy' marriage system (marriage between a female of lower cultural heredity and a male of higher cultural heredity), the 'caste' of lower-rank females could climb up to a higher caste rank. *[Source: Human Genome and Indian Caste System; 'The Asian Age', London - 30/04/1998]*

However, very interestingly, this natural law of genetic-lift had been followed in every human society, and accordingly, the marriage system was established. Their life experiences forced them to consciously reject 'in-breeding' and 'hypogamy' (between stronger females and weaker males from a hereditary point of view), and marriage to protect and progress mankind. But the most important social event of adopting leadership in social life came up for better social-becoming at the beginning of human society. Worldwide human beings in their respective groups selected a leader of more wisdom and capability, who would guide and lead them to overcome hostile forces and to win the battle of life. The same is also found in the social system prevailing in the families of different groups of animals. But, unfortunately, now in the name of so-called people's liberty, the value of selective breeding (genetically compatible marriage) for human existence is being compromised!

Loving Attachment: Initiation

We know there is a centre of the universe; the sun is the centre of attachment of the existence of the solar system; the nucleus is the centre of the existence of a cell. So, from the micro to the macro level, life exists in concentric attachment. It also persists in humans, as he is the product of the urge for the unification of sex cells, sperm and ovum.

On the path of social evolution, human beings always search for such personalities from whom they could be guided and inspired to overcome the struggle of being and becoming and may form a better society. When people with diverse characteristics unite around a centre, then their collective concentration stimulates their innate tendency for fulfilment. Thus, advanced societies gradually emerged through people's mutual fulfilment, driven by Ideal-centric motivation. And the normal social economy also grew to protect and nurture the individual's fulfilling nature with this democratic social mechanism.

At the beginning of human society, there were natural leaders. The loving attachment of individuals towards these leaders led them to explore the environment to collect attributes to evolve. Since the thinking and working process of man is handled by his complexes like lust, anger, greed, etc., his centre and intensity of attachment rearrange these complexes to fulfil the wants of his loving centre. Thus, if the centre of attachment to love is a man of the materialised form of godly qualities and wisdom, then obviously unregulated complexes would be systematically organised to elevate him to the peak of an integrated personality and a man of efficiency. Hence, people naturally gather around great leaders. So, the root of all kinds of mass movements is virtually a 'personality-centred' movement. Psychologically speaking, the inherent hankering of the human being is to remain attached to any man, whether he is a matter or material. According to the father of Psychology, Freud, the inborn 'libido', i.e., the normal tendency of attachment of man when he gets inclined towards a 'psychologist' or a self-controlled person, then he (psychic patient) gradually becomes normal and balanced. As a corollary, the attachment of one's libido to the psychoanalyst makes his complications meaningfully adjusted.

He connected this natural human tendency of loving attachment (libido) to the integrated personality of a realised Ideal-man. He called this indispensable process of human existence "Initiation". In this course, He introduced the latest and most refined scientific process of meditation (a psycho-spiritual technique to make the neurological & psychic system sensitive & ordered) for the whole of mankind, which reveals the path of total consciousness to realise the quests of life. This technique is conveyed in the process of Initiation. So, true and meaningful self-realisation starts only with Initiation.

Studying the effects of people's movements, it is found that comparatively *'Dharma'*-oriented movements - the mass mobilisation of the culture of being and becoming under the leadership of the world spiritual Seers - are more successful in influencing the larger mass, consistently for a longer period. It was possible because people found a comparatively better living expression of existential ideology among these extremely self-adjusted personalities, more than the leaders of the other socio-political movements. Thus, they discovered the path of life and growth - the ultimate desire to adjust their complexes in better ways. Sree Sree Anukulchandra says - Sree Krishna, Gautama Buddha, Jesus Christ, Hazrat Mohammad, Sree Chaitanya, and Sree Ramakrishna are such personalities who have modified the same *'Dharma'* (the Aryan culture of life-growth) as per the people's existing mental and material conditions and requirements of the contemporary societies. So, each of them is the fulfiller of the past Seers, because they are all the cultivators of the 'Aryan' culture of existentialism or upholders of *'Dharma'*. Sree Sree Anukulchandra also says, "The way of upholding the urge of our existence is *Dharma*." He explains - "*Dharma* never becomes many.....Hindu *Dharma*, Christian *Dharma*, Mohammedan *Dharma*, Buddhist *Dharma,* etc., are wrong; rather, they are so many views." His view – 'the degeneration of humanity began when people deviated from the path of the life of the Seers'. Without 'libido' toward the latest and past fulfillers or social Seers, people's progress becomes de-centred, leading to increased unadjusted complexes and abnormal tendencies. These forces drag the social (economic, political, cultural, moral, etc.) progress and unity downwards and, at the same time, encourage communalism, separatism, provincialism, exploitation, and various other evil practices in society.

Self-Realisation: Education

Sree Sree Anukulchandra, as the latest Seer said – "The systematic organisation of habits and instincts to fulfil the becoming of life, by graduated active manipulation of behaviour, may be called Education" *[Nana Prasange/Vol-3].* Instinct refers to the inherent genetic character that arises from within, while habit is the tendency of repetitive personal activities. The purpose of education is to regulate these towards the existence and becoming of individuals and the environment. The inner sense is designed to build character and develop efficiency, enabling individuals to navigate and influence the socio-environmental system in favour of existence and life's continuous becoming. This learning process starts with a loving attachment to the Master-man who has total command over all the matters and faculties of knowledge. Basic education takes place at home under divine, conjugal, and family life, as one can become a 'disciplined' person by being a 'disciple' of Master-man. Regard and respect for guides play a crucial role in an individual's education.

Therefore, leaders such as teachers, parents, or social workers must have a superior beloved - a man of wisdom, in their lives. It makes the right interrelationships of different faculties of knowledge and the know-how of manipulating them for the greater cause of life to keep the balance in a socio-environmental ecological system. This Ideal-centric education cultivates wisdom, integrity, and a spirit of inquisitive service toward the environment. Thus, true education is self-realisation, which grants mastery over the entire system, fostering a mindset conducive to scientific research, household industry, self-reliance, a people-driven economy, reduced unemployment, and the strength to thrive in global competition, etc. Another important aspect is that education nurtures inborn instincts; however, for the emergence of better instincts, reformed genetic-lift becomes essential and indispensable.

Psychogenic Evolution: Marriage Reform

Through long experience, human beings observed that random selection of males and females does not always result in qualitatively better offspring. So human beings opted for some laws. **Firstly,** they prohibited marriage between nearer blood relations. This has now become a 'law' in many countries. **Secondly**, they found that breeding between the male of less bio-cultural-heredity (lower Varna) and the female of higher bio-cultural-heredity, i.e., in hypogamy (*pratilom*) marriage, generation devolves and degenerates in terms of characteristics and potentialities. Sree Sree Anukulchandra states: "Marriage between a more evolved female and a less evolved male ('hypogamous' breeding) typically results in offspring with a rebellious nature, so for the sake of human existence, practising of 'hypogamy' should be strictly prohibited through proper education of psychogenic-lift science, especially to the girls." Interestingly, modern scientists follow the same principles in crop and animal breeding to produce high-yielding seeds and healthier offspring. He also says, "Marriage between a male and female could only take place if they have 'biological' and 'psychological' compatibility. Thus, females of lower cultural heredity will be culturally and biologically upgraded." Dr James Watson, the father of modern genetics and a Nobel Prize winner, acknowledged the hereditary advancement inherent in the Indo-Aryan marriage system, based on the very social structure (*Varna* system), and the DNA tests of 'caste' characters excellently support the nature of *this division* and its' progressive purpose of the traditional marriage system. *[86th Indian Science Congress]*

The practice of the most reformed culture (Brahminism) across generations in the Varna system, under the guidance of a 'Seer', enables everyone (even the so-called backwards class) to acquire refined genetically transmittable instincts that promote higher social rank. Because genetically, there is a minor (less than 1%) difference among the different instinctive classes. In this context, Swami Vivekananda also said, "Everyone (of all *Varna*) has to be Brahmin".

Anukulchandra's concept of marriage introduces a new approach to Human Resource Development (HRD). This law is also found in chemical reactions and the cross-breeding of the plant and animal kingdoms. Only selective mating on genetic matching of males and females gives qualitatively better offspring. So, the purpose of marriage has twofold goals: **(1)** self-becoming and **(2)** producing better progeny, both of which are achievable through selective mating on genetic compatibility. In nature, the laws of chemical and biological reproduction suggest that - when a female (-ve) with higher hereditary instincts meets with a male (+ve) with lower hereditary instincts, - the offspring fails to inherit the superior qualities of the parent, resulting in psychogenic imbalance. So, scientists have rejected this system (Hypogamy) of breeding. Sree Sree Anukulchandra also opposes this marriage(?) to stop the birth of 'destructive nature' offspring, which seriously harms social evolution, and significantly, this science of genetic-lift was conceptualised by the ancient Aryan Seers first time more than 8000 years ago!

The natural law of genetic-lift (often called *eugenics*) stands on psychogenic compatibility, which is needed for making a relationship between opposite sexes for marriage. Here, the privilege of mate selection is primarily bestowed on a female. She would be trained (educated) enough to select the best one (mate) for herself in terms of better heredity, culture, efficiency, character, health, etc., whom she can love from within forever. She should reject the male who entices and offers girls for love-making. This higher-loving and regardful tension of a girl towards her lover makes her the mother of a higher soul, along with happy, everlasting conjugal love. Such reformation in marriage begets the psychogenetic evolution of mankind, which fructifies overall peace in the families, thereby encompassing every sphere of society. Western scientists also proved this law for human potential management in terms of genetic and psychic compatibility for mate selection. But few discard any 'restriction' over free relationships and the 'selective breeding' concept in the name of 'violation of human rights'! So, we should realise the essence of the 'science of genetic-lifting' as a crucial factor in selection, and its deep impact on human existence.

Foundation of Human Existence:

Throughout world history, many civilisations have risen and fallen. According to the vision of the Master of the Age, the destruction of civilisations can be attributed to the lack of Ideal-centric integration and the prevalence of unchecked, abnormal sexual relationships. **Initiation** fosters self-adjustment for a concentric and purposeful life, **Education** stimulates inner virtuous instincts, and **Marriage Reform** aims to cultivate better genetic qualities in offspring, aligned with a harmonious conjugal life. These three factors are crucial for maintaining the stability of an individual's mental and biological constitution. The Master (the greatest prophet and lover of humanity) asserts that reforming these vital man-making factors will safeguard human civilisation and gradually elevate it into a superior world society — a 'divine communism' in terms of the 'World United States' (**WUS**).

Hence, under the guidance of the latest Seer, who is the fulfiller of the past incarnations of Seers or prophets, fostering a concentric, inter-fulfilling attitude will unify humanity, strengthening collective harmony and purpose. And then they (united strength) will find the scientific solutions which will root out all barriers and obstacles on their way to have real peace, bliss, and progress in every sphere of life. According to Him, this will fulfil humanity's eternal quest to 'be and become' - a vision He has pursued since the very beginning of His mission to uplift mankind.

Indo-Aryanization: A Silent Revolution

The individual is the building block of society. The gradual awakening of divinity within an individual's psychic and mental constitution is the driving force of social evolution. Indo-Aryanization is a cultural movement aimed at elevating individual and collective life to uphold global humanity, initiated by the Aryan Seers over 8000 years ago. The objective of this movement is to bring everyone under the fold of the culture of existence based on one's cultural heritage, such as religion, belief, thought, practice, habit, instinct, etc. As part of this program of Indo-Aryanization, the fundamental principles of IndoAryan Existentialism manifest through accepting the Ideal's guidance (Initiation), cultivating inner virtues (Education), and adhering to the natural laws of cultural heredity, including *Varnashram* and scientific 'marriage-reform'. These programs need to be popularised among individuals in the world by avoiding any kind of confrontation and hostility. This is not a political, communal, or racial movement, but the movement of existence and evolution of the entire humanity.

Thousands of years ago, these truths of human existence were first discovered by a group of enlightened sages known as the Aryan Seers. Later on, these facts were carried away by the next Aryan world teachers, including Sree Rama, Sree Krishna, Gautama Buddha, Jesus Christ, Hazrat Mohammad, Sree Chaitanya, Sree Ramakrishna, Sree Sree Anukulchandra, etc. Regrettably, in the last century, the concept of 'Aryanism' was distorted and misused by certain fascist ideologies, obscuring its true essence in terms of racist discrimination! However, by reviving this movement, Indo-Aryan culture can be restored to its rightful place as a guiding social principle, harmonising with the universal laws of evolution, with communal harmony following the 'Saptarchi', i.e. the seven-point rules of Indo-Aryanization, which are: **(1)** God is one, and all Prophets are the messengers of the same. **(2)** The latest Prophet is the fulfiller of the past. **(3)** Everyone (communities) should accept the latest Prophet as the incarnation of the past, to modernise their belief. **(4)** Forefathers should be sincerely regarded. **(5)** Past enlightened personalities (*Devta*) shouldn't be neglected. **(6)** Psycho-genic traits of a grouping of hereditary instincts should be preserved and evolved. **(7)** The law of genetic-lift must be followed, and at the utmost, hypogamy relation (female of superior heredity, lesser male) should be stopped, to protect against severe loss potentials.

Then, this movement will be spread into the global sphere by conforming to the universal laws of evolution. This psychogenic transformation of individuals is an inevitable process of the 'silent revolution' of Indo-Aryanisation to evolve into a divine world society, i.e., Indo-Aryan communism, which is the ultimate destination of social evolution. Indo-Aryan communism envisions a global village of highly conscious individuals, embodying Brahminic qualities, who instinctively perceive oneness in all aspects of the ecological system and actively work to sustain the equilibrium of existence and becoming. This is 'Indo-Aryan Globalisation'.

Thus, 'Aryan Globalisation' represents the ancient discovery of human evolutionary laws, designed to balance the socio-environmental ecology (SEE) of modern civilisation through the realisation of universal oneness.

Divine Global Society:

Communism is the highest phase of the socio-political system. This society can be developed by the most bio-culturally advanced people, as viewed by many of the great thinkers like Aristotle, Socrates, Plato, Homer, Karl Marx, etc., since the beginning of civilisation. Sree Sree Anukulchandra focused on this matter in terms of "Indo-Aryan-Communism". According to Him, the basis of Aryan Communism stands on the distribution of work according to the instinctive and hereditary character of individuals. He explains that under the leadership of an all-fulfilling Ideal personality in Indo-Aryan-socialism, human beings will uphold and nurture the division of labour according to hereditary instinct or evolutionary division of social labour. The purpose of this socio-political system is to promote a qualitative transformation of each individual into a bio-culturally superior class ('Brahmin'), solving modern socio-economic problems. 'Brahmins' are culturally and hereditarily the most advanced people and engaged with the cultivation of the culture of existentialism to serve the surroundings.

Indo-Aryan socialist economy stands, where ownership of the wealth will neither go to the state, nor will it be controlled by the corporates; rather economy will be handled by the common people under the industrial ownership. Instead, big industries will be distributed among the family-based small-scale industries to encourage direct individual involvement, which enables scientific research work for qualitative development and alternative resources, growth of a self-reliant economy to be a deciding factor in a globalised economy, along with the definite elimination of poverty and unemployment. Accordingly, an application and industry-based System should be structured. So, basic needs (law, infrastructure, power, etc) should be properly managed by the selected people's government.

Hence, Indo-Aryan Socialism could be transformed into a divine 'Aryan Communism' by this 'cultural and hereditary qualitative change' of the people, and this concept is very much refined and evolved over the so-called Marxist communism. According to Sree Sree Anukulchandra, this 'culture of life and growth' is 'IndoAryan-culture'. So, *Dharma* can be interpreted as the scientific culture of life and growth that will be acceptable to everybody, and the IndoAryan culture would appear as the 'culture of existentialism' for all. So, *Dharma* can't be many; it is one, and society can't be *'Dharma Nirapeksha'* (secular), and there is not a single 'non-communal Dharmik' to be found in the society. Thus, by following the path of *'Dharma'* of life and growth as shown by the latest 'Fulfiller the Best', all the inter-interested nations of the world can dissolve the formal boundaries of the states, and they will come together to form one Global Nation, the model of which is – "World United States" (WUS).

Dharma and Science:

The latest view of *'Dharma'*, as given by Sree Sree Anukulchandra, cannot be bracketed with the general concept of *Dharma* or Religion as practised in society, which consists of rituals, mundane utterances of psalms with the accompaniment of the burning of incense daily, which was solely based on 'fear'. To put it simply, the notion of religion, in the common parlance, appeared as a non-materialistic go-of-life. Sree Sree Anukulchandra has put forward the view that every person can be a *Dharmik,* even without believing in God existence. 'God' is nothing but the 'existential urge' of matter, which exists as the cause of evolution. He conveyed that any living particle, first of all, wants to exist and then also wants to evolve. It means that it has a tremendous desire to be and become. So, the best method to fulfil and appropriate the desire of this life and growth is called 'Dharma'; in other words, the science of being and becoming is Dharma. So, by maintaining the livelihood, one somehow follows Dharma, but the means one takes recourse to maintain one's existence, one gets the reward accordingly. The notion is that one mustn't ignore the existence of his environment for self-becoming. Modern applied science is evolving due to the desire for a better existence of life, i.e. due to *Dharma*, science is coming to fruition. Hence, *Dharma* has been in progress since the beginning of life and the ever-advancing march of science since the beginning of human civilisation. Thus, only '*Dharma*' encourages socio-cultural success and scientific-technological development, and in the long run, it would be translated into reality, that due to *Dharma* (the desire of Being and Becoming), this headway of life will continue and usher in another new phase. The best demonstrator of *Dharma* is He who demonstrates the best technique of adjustment of human complexes, which is advantageous to being and becoming. They are called Prophets of humanity or Aryan Seers or World teachers such as Krishna, Buddha, Jesus, Mohammad, Chaitanya, Ramakrishna, etc. They carried forward their missionary activities and transcended the notion of complexes for the entire humanity according to the socio-cultural situation of the contemporary ages. So, there is no difference between them in terms of the science of life.

Materialism and Spiritualism:

As Dharma and science are interrelated, it is similarly found that materialism and spiritualism are also interdependent, as matter is the condensed form of energy. In this way, energy is the spirit of matter. Spiritual life means the "cause-finding go-of-life," involving a realisation of oneness with the whole, marked by an unrepelling adherence to the Master-man. On the other hand, the material way of life involves analytical and reasoning-based progress toward the root of facts by manipulating matter for human benefit. Spiritual practices stand on psycho-physical exercises that refine our nervous system, enhancing the capacity to receive and reciprocate impulses from existential factors in our surroundings. This heightened awareness leads to benevolent mastery over existential-mechanism, which is essentially 'God-realization.'

Hence, without spiritualism, materialism cannot flourish; in other words, true success in the material world is incomplete without a spiritual life because it takes us to the root cause. By applying spiritual techniques in humans and increasing sensitivity, one realises the truths of nature and its relationship with the larger and immediate environment. Since humans have evolved from the same fundamental elements as the universe, they can connect with their surroundings through spiritual practices. As a result, individuals naturally cultivate qualities like love, cooperation, and compassion, unlocking the secrets of success in material life. Sree Sree Anukulchandra says: "Spirit is that which makes the matter materially stay from behind it. The matter has fine-to-fine states. As we go ahead, we find finer layers... A condensed form of energy (spirit) matters... the Existential-urge is present in the matter, as the cause of ecological evolution – is **God**"

He thinks 'to know God' is to unfold the causes behind events. Thus, exploring the interrelationship within the universal ecosystem through realisation is, in essence, the science of spirituality, and who understands the mechanism of macrocosmic ecological balance and can harness science for better human existence may be called a 'Human God.'

His prescribed initiation of the 'latest technique of meditation' has made this opportunity accessible to all. Significantly, Sree Sree Anukulchandra emphasises: "True material development means spiritual development and spiritual development means necessary material development."

Socio-Environmental-Ecology (SEE):

The above-mentioned factors are very significant laws of evolutionary nature and the rule of social evolution derived using synthesis and analysis of natural and social progress. These laws are based on the systemic application of the natural process of evolution of the universe in human society. It organises the excellent balance between matter, life, and human beings. In the background of nature's (inorganic and organic) evolution, the material and spiritual development of the human being has taken place. From this (material and spiritual) point of view, a human being's efficiency, labour, as well as his thought, intellect, realisation, and the socio-economy, get synchronised to build up a new mechanism. This mechanism may be called Socio-Environmental-Ecology (SEE).

Now, to balance this ecology, human beings have to uphold the laws of the evolution of nature. The human being, as the finest specimen of the long evolution of nature, can realise his integral relationship with this whole universal mechanism.

He also has the full potential to achieve the 'feeling of oneness' with the totality. This realisation comes to be translated into reality when he gets attached to 'One' – the Man of total consciousness. These faculties are inherent in human beings. Hence, these laws are exceptionally relevant to protect, nurture, and progress humankind. So, the mission of man-making is to uphold humanity. To build a genuinely true, peaceful, and ever-progressive world by qualitative psychogenic (bio-psychic units) evolution of each individual, an integral link between the past and the present is indispensable. So, the whole program should be founded on the three pillars of natural and social evolution. Conclusively, the pillars are: **(1)** Concentric go-of-life under the leadership of a man of wisdom, i.e. centralised motion, **(2)** Nourishment of inner instinct of the individual to unfold efficiency, i.e., unfolding potentials, and **(3)** Psychogenic reform to have better progeny, i.e., genetic becoming. These pillars were termed by Sree Sree Anukulchandra as **(1)** Initiation, **(2)** Education, and **(3)** Marriage. Now these must stand on the strong plinth of well-managed 'Evolutionary division of social labour' which is also called by Him as a true *Varnashram*, which is not man-made, but rather discovered by the wise men, i.e. Seers or Rishis, keenly observing the cause of the progress of nature and society.

Realisation of 'Oneness':

This is a scientific fact, and it is also supported by most of the spiritual scriptures like The Vedas, The Bible, The Quran, etc., and the staple truth being enunciated in these texts is that at the beginning there was 'One' – the single unit. This whole universal system has evolved from that single 'unit', and even now, it continues to evolve following the same systematic natural process of existential-becoming. Each of us is a product of this creation, which was initiated from that One. Thus, we have an integral relationship with this universal system to keep our existence. That is the reason why every life has an inner tendency to be unified with the 'One', having the realisation of the feeling of 'Oneness' with the whole. This tendency of unification is present in all of the matters in nature, as an existential force. In the macro system, the movement of the solar system or the celestial bodies in the universe has a concentric circular progression around the centre in different layers. Finally, its life comes to an end, collapses, and merges into its central body.

In the microform, each cell or atom is concentrated with its central nucleus, and the existence of matter (a combined form of atoms) stands on a well-balanced, mutual systematic networking of atoms. The entire matter and life together make a magnificent balance of the ecosystem to live together, fostering the sustained evolution of the entire system. This natural course of togetherness with the feeling of oneness in this variegated world is one of the mandatory events to live and grow, and this natural togetherness proves that there is an inherent bending of 'realisation of the feeling of Oneness' in each of us. So, we notice that there is 'unity in diversity'. It proves that the laws of the universal ecosystem work in human life as well, to uphold its existence and to continue the pulse of becoming.

Secret of Infinite Consciousness:

The electronic state is the finer state of matter following our present knowledge. In every atom, electrons move in a regular orbit around the nucleus. So, in every atom, there is a variation of moving electrons, and there is also a variation of vibration (movement). If the number of electrons changes, the structure and characteristics of matter also change simultaneously. So, a variety of vibrations becomes the cause of variations in the character of matter. It is a well-established fact that the universe originated from a massive explosion (vibration) at the beginning of the creation of the universe, and all the spiritual scriptures of the world, such as the Vedas, the Bible, the Quran, etc., also concretise the same incident that science believes. Similarly, human consciousness and intelligence also vary according to the rhythm of life ('inner song'). If we could find the right scientific technique for infusing the finest level of sound or vibration within our psycho-physical system, it might change the whole mechanism of our body, mind, and nervous system, which would cause a change in the total personality. The latest Master Sree Sree Anukulchandra has revealed the easiest and the latest technique of practising the scientific technique of meditation for mankind, irrespective of any religion, caste, creed, colour, or region, and which is the condensed form of all past processes of spiritual practice (*Sadhana*). The efficacious characteristics of Sadhana can be elaborated by three different heads in the following manner. **Firstly,** everyone, irrespective of any belief and cultural heritage, can realise the relevance of the truth of their faith in the contemporary age. **Secondly**, it intensifies the analytical and perception power of the brain and nervous system, which finds the secrets of the mechanism of the balance of the interrelationships of matters in the creation, in terms of one's total existential evolution. It means that it can reveal one's path of the journey since the beginning (creation) and evolve the feeling of 'oneness' with the totality. **Thirdly,** the most important fact is that it reorganises the human complexes in an orderly manner, explores maximum inner potentials towards existential-becoming, and minimises the wastage of energy as well. It is open to everyone to accept this easiest, innovative, and outstanding 'Sadhana' that works in two-tier directions. Simultaneously, it is psychic manipulation and imparting specific vibrations to evolve into super-consciousness. Therefore, a sense of togetherness at the highest level of spiritual realisation and material analysis impels one to become a perfect, authentic human being. He plays the foremost role to: *"Conserve the balance of evolving mechanism of socio-universal eco-system and realise the feeling of Oneness with the totality...!"*

Law of Success and Happiness:

The following disciplines constitute the Law of Success and Happiness. These are: **(1)** Keeping the physical (hygienic), mental (complex adjustment), and spiritual (concentric go-of-life) health in order, **(2)** Getting mastery over the urge of complexes, divert them towards becoming of life, **(3)** Acting promptly to manifest positive impulses in reality, **(4)** The performance of the inquisitive service to the environment to fulfill the wishes of the living Master, **(5)** Avoiding 'Go-between' *(not keeping words, misuse of money for other specific use,... makes one a man of dual personality with conflicting complexes)*, and **(6)** 'Libido-distortion' *(The constant refusal in the attempt to get the desired thing which one strongly wants makes one undergo a certain amount of nonchalance which ultimately impairs the libido which can be defined as a tendency towards the centripetal entity.)*

IndoAryan Existentialism:

Indo-Aryanism is **(1)** the division of Characters and grouping of matter and life, **(2)** the centralised motion of the universe, atom, and concentric life with self-realisation, and **(3)** the specific law of multiplication of matter and psychogenic-lift.

Existentialism is a systematic and constructive urge to exist, which is: **(1)** The primary desire of life is to exist and evolve, **(2)** Maintaining the balance of the socio-environmental ecosystem to live and grow, and **(3)** the Revelation of the consciousness of 'Oneness' with the universal ecosystem in terms of total evolution.

IndoAryan Man Making Mission (IM3):

The ten-point protocols of the Indo-Aryan Man-Making Mission (IM3) stand on the three pillars of the 'IndoAryan Existentialism', i.e. Initiation, Education, Eugenics (IEE) and hold the most essential universal factors of total being and becoming of mankind, the foundation of nation-building and a divine World order. Those key points are:

1. Innate Urge: Each matter has an 'existential urge' - the life throb. It wants to live and grow to keep its existence expanding. Such an urge in humans makes them conscious and active in controlling the environment for existence. This prime driving force of the evolution of matter is called 'Goodness'. Hence, our final goal is the realisation of existence.

2. Ever Lasting Torch: In the course of life, to explore the inherent possibilities to their maximum degree and to apply profitably the material possibilities with all-inclusive spiritual knowledge profitably, we need a man of wisdom or a realised living Master. Such a personality as a human is 'God' himself, whose directions are inevitable to overcome all sorts of hurdles in the existential evolution of mankind.

3. All-in-One: Hence, God - 'the existential urge of matter' is One. Dharma - 'the science of existential evolution' is One. And all world-teachers or Prophets are the messengers of the same (One God & One Dharma).

4. Nature's Lesson: The result of the biochemical and socio-cultural evolution is a grouping of similar characteristics of matter, followed by the division of labour according to the hereditary instincts among various species. Significantly, the same phenomena have also occurred in human beings. So, a hereditary grouping of similar characteristics of humans should be protected and nurtured to transform individuals towards their highest grade of characteristics for the progress of civilisation.

5.　Lift Law: Application of the natural laws of psychogenic-lift, based on a grouping of hereditary instincts, would procure a better instinctive human resource by birth. On the contrary, awareness has to be built up to reject or restrict anti-natural *'hypogamous'* marriage (mating between higher instinctive females and less evolved males). A strong action program should be initiated to stop such marriages and to prevent a great loss of human potential and global humanity. All must be connected to the Ideal-centric life, aligned to the living embodiment of a higher purpose of existence, to make a harmonious, conjugal, and peaceful family environment, a building block of a global society.

6.　Self-Discovery: The education system has to be modified with 'elevated intellectualism'. Here, knowledge must be introduced based on practical and industrial education, since the primary level is imparted by the disciplined teachers, who are disciples of the realised Master. This would reveal the cause-and-effect relationship of all-natural phenomena, and show the right application of knowledge to fulfil social needs and also unfurl the intersubject relation, which would open wisdom.

7.　Social Change: Such educational enrichment would help humans to be transformed into a socialist society that is free from unemployment, poverty, economic crisis, industrial downfall, unhealthy competition, capitalistic exploitation, state autocracy, loss of human resources, economic dependency, social discrimination, etc. And the state would come forward to play a leading role in the globalised economy. An economy sprouting up from such a system will only proliferate the ecology. The Indo-Aryan Soviet Socialist Republic (IASSR) is a model of such a socio-economic divine-democratic political structure of future greater India, extending it to the new humanitarian world order.

8. People's Power: True democracy comes from the representatives of the conscious and qualitatively better psycho-genic human resource, which is free from 'party politics' and runs under the guidance of the man of wisdom or the Ideal. So, in this alternative dynamic system, there will be no nominee, no political party, no police force, and no huge expenditure; but it comes from one representative from each family, who would select the best one from the village or ward. Such village representatives will select the best one at the district level. They would select the best representative at the state level. And from there, the country would get the best group of leaders to lead the country progressively.

9. Global Move: The go-of-life of total becoming with the togetherness of humanity and all fulfilling ideology is called 'IndoAryan Existentialism'. It has an inherent potential to shape the world. Its mission is to transform each individual into the highest level of psychogenic characteristics (a *'Brahmin' by character*). This is possible by following the fundamental program of human development, inspired by the theme of Indo-Aryanism. This was dreamed of and began in practice by the ancient Aryan Seers to make a divine global society. This mission would lay a strong foundation for a unanimous *Dharmik* world order, having supportive coordination among the countries, following the leadership of a common all-fulfilling Ideal. This is the background of the future World United States (WUS), the divine *Communism*.

10. A Total Ecology: Human existence is directly connected to the coordination among the biophysical existential urges of life. 'Everyone is essential for my existence' – this awareness auto-initiatively inspires to protect, nurture, and balance the socio-environmental-ecology (SEE). In such a go-of-life under the leadership of the Master, one gradually discovers his relationship with the total mechanism and attainment of self-realisation with a feeling of oneness with all. This realisation is the ultimate goal of life.

Conclusion:

This is an outcome of Ph.D.-awarded research work that explores the relevance of Indo-Aryan culture in modern times, showing its potential to unify diverse spiritual, material, and philosophical ideologies from East and West on a shared platform for human perfection. This book is a summary of the book "*Relevance of the Ideology of Sree Sree Anukulchandra in Modern Society – A Sociological Analysis*", based on PhD work. It introduces the Indo-Aryan view of Existentialism as a transformative ideology, aiming to create a new world order through the psychogenic evolution of individuals into divine beings and promoting global humanity, unity, and prosperity.

The study identifies Sree Sree Anukulchandra seems to be one of the World Masters, continuing the legacy of ancient Aryan seers forward. His works are serious enough to be included in the UG and PG course of studies of all branches of Social Sciences to enrich an all-around innovative mind to see the world, and exclusive research works are needed to excavate the hidden enormous treasure in his ideology, for which the world is looking to solve geo-political and socio-economic problems across the Globe.

His century-old movement, now carried advancing by various groups and organisations, must unite under His documented ideological guidelines to prevent societal degeneration and guide to uphold its values through the growing existential darkness.

Aryanism: *An ancient discovery of the science of human existence*
Soviet: *Council of the Union of local representatives*
Communism: *Comm + Une: Connected to one: Common 'Ism'*
Brahmin: *Those who have acquired wisdom - the laws of existence*
Bipra: *Those carry Brahminic character as biological heredity*

About the author

Dr Srikumar Mukherjee, the author of this book, is a state-level 'Best Teacher' awarded teacher, teaching Information Technology in Delhi Public School, SAIL Township, Ranchi, India. He is passionately involved as a 'Life & Lift Tutor' in an educational movement, "IndoAryan Man Making Mission" (IM3), aiming to make a better psychogenic mankind. He is the founder of the open-source virtual school 'IndoAryan School of H.R.D.' (ISHRD) to educate people about "IndoAryan Existentialism", which is an outcome of his research (PhD) work in Sociology, a new revelation in the field of HRD. He voluntarily serves in Psycho-Spiritual healing as an authorised instructor (SPR) and also an editor-publisher of an e-paper "The IndoARYAN Existentialism"

For further details, please contact

IndoAryan School of H.R.D.
Cell# +91- 9470932544 / 8210137153
Email: srikumar.hrm@gmail.com
Website: **www**[dot]**indoaryan**[dot]**in**

<u>A few other books by the author</u>

- **Science of Education** – *A Handbook for Parents, Teachers & Students*

- **Existential Quest** – *A key to life and lift*

- **IndoAryan Culture** – *A Historical Document of Global Consciousness*

- **Relevance of the Ideology of Sree Sree Anukulchandra in Modern Society** - *A Sociological Analysis*

- **Python for Beginners**: *The Easy Guide to Coding & Data Science*

- আর্যকৃষ্টি: *বিশ্বচেতনার এক ঐতিহাসিক দলিল*

- आर्यकृष्टि: *विश्व चेतना का एक ऐतिहासिक खोज*

- युवाचेतना और जीवनवृद्धिवाद

- श्रीश्रीअनुकूलचन्द्र के जीवनवृद्धिवादी सिद्धान्त का मूलतत्त्व: *एक समाज वैज्ञानिक अध्ययन*

www.ingramcontent.com/pod-product-compliance
Lightning Source LLC
Chambersburg PA
CBHW020653160726
47991CB00003B/1162